The Tiny
Warrior

The Tiny Warrior

A PATH TO
PERSONAL
DISCOVERY AND
ACHIEVEMENT

D. J. Eagle Bear Vanas

Andrews McMeel
PUBLISHING®

Andrews McMeel Publishing
a division of Andrews McMeel Universal
1130 Walnut Street, Kansas City, Missouri 64106

www.andrewsmcmeel.com

18 19 20 21 22 SDB 22 21 20 19 18

ISBN: 978-0-7407-3388-8

Library of Congress Catalog Control Number: 2002035626

Book composition by Kelly & Company

Dedication

To THE CREATOR, who is always guiding us if we only listen.

To my parents, Darrell and Mary Jo Vanas, who taught me to dream big and believe in myself. They spent their lives blessing me with unconditional love, discipline and leadership by example. You're my greatest heroes.

To Mrs. Caranna, my high school English teacher, who ignited a passion in me for writing.

To my beautiful wife, Arienne—my muse, my soul mate and my coach and advisor on this project. I couldn't have done this without your support. I love you.

To my daughter, Gabrielle—my greatest gift. She melts all my worries away with a smile and inspires me each day, allowing me to watch a real "tiny warrior" grow.

To my Uncle Tony, you are always with me. Thank you for teaching me to appreciate the gifts of life, love and laughter.

To the victims who perished on September 11, 2001, and to the friends and families they left behind. The world watched warriors in action, from Flight 93 to the streets of New York City to the halls of the Pentagon, as they sacrificed themselves to serve others. You will always be remembered . . .

Contents

Preface

POW! I heard the chokecherry sticks rip from my chest like firecrackers and watched the ropes attached to them fly away from me. My knees were weak, but my spirit soared. I looked down to see blood pouring past my red felt skirt and staining the dusty ground . . .

It was the summer of 1997, and I was on Pine Ridge Reservation in southern South Dakota going through my fourth year of the Lakota Sun Dance ceremony. Sun Dance is an ancient traditional ceremony conducted outdoors on a rural piece of nature. It is done away from the hustle of everyday life so participants can better connect with the Creator.

I could hear the pulse of the drum and smell burning sage hanging thickly in the air. I could feel the blistering heat on my skin, the cactus needles in my feet and hot dust in the back of my throat. When my spiritual leader approached, he grabbed my sage bracelet and ran with me around the inside of the large sacred circle of tobacco ties, which formed the center of the Sun Dance grounds.

For four years, I had prepared for this very moment. Now that it had arrived, he didn't say "good job" or "congratulations." He simply said, "You are a warrior now." For me, it wasn't a moment of pride, but a moment of extreme humility. I felt about an inch tall. I knew that being a warrior was not for personal glory; it was a call to serve others.

The Lakota people practice the Sun Dance for four days each summer to show respect and honor to White Buffalo Calf Maiden, the spirit that brought the gift of the prayer pipe. On the third day, future warriors undergo the "piercing" to show respect to mothers of the world for enduring the pain of childbirth.

During the ceremony, we lie on a buffalo robe next to the large cottonwood "tree of life" while elders insert skewers made of chokecherry wood the size of ink pens into our chests. The skewers are fastened to a one-hundred-foot length of rope. The rope is then tied to the tree, which represents our connection to the Creator. Ultimately, we pull backward until we rip away. Then, we're "set free" by the Creator, leaving our ignorance and our former selves behind.

Sun Dance also helps us show thanksgiving for the things we take for granted—such as food, water and family—by requiring that we go without them. During these four days, Sun Dancers also sacrifice their comfort to pray for the health, happiness and success of all people throughout the world.

Much of the inspiration for this book has stemmed from the unique things I experienced during my four years of sun dancing. For instance, I learned what the warrior path was truly about, which had nothing to do with what I had seen in movies, heard in music or read in books. It wasn't about being destructive or the toughest person in the neighborhood or any other media-stained image. In my moments of terror, pain and loneliness, I realized that this ceremony wasn't self-serving.

Rather, the warrior concept simply asks that we develop our own talent and ability so we can serve and defend others. The warrior's goal is to become an asset to the village he serves. Native American notables like Pontiac, Crazy Horse, Chief Joseph and Tecumseh were warriors not only because of their exploits in battle. They were also warriors because they made great personal sacrifices to lead their people during times of extreme danger, to work tirelessly developing other warriors and tactics and to negotiate for the survival of their people.

The warrior path transcends race, gender and age. It can be followed by anyone willing. So, today *your* "village" could be your family, community, country, campus, coworkers or clients. Ask yourself, "What am I doing to become an asset to the village I serve?"

After all, every day you face challenges at home, work, school or within yourself. When you allow your tiny warrior to emerge, you can learn to consistently overcome these challenges and obtain the happiness and success you desire and deserve. Remember, your progress and fulfillment in life at any point in time is in exact balance to how much you're helping others achieve the same.

In a constantly changing world, the traditional warrior concept remains unchanged. Inside each person a powerful and positive force exists, an unfathomable beauty and limitless pool of talent and ability. Inside each one of us, a tiny warrior waits to be discovered. If you have the courage to let him or her out, you can truly live the life of your dreams.

Acknowledgments

I AM GRATEFUL to the many people who have helped me on my life journey. They are the ones who ultimately helped me create this book. My most heartfelt thanks go to:

My amazing sister, Kimberly, for being my friend, cheerleader and the best sister in the world.

My teachers Patty Caranna, Susan Hunt, Nancy Hunter and Richard Belvel for seeing talent in me before I saw it in myself.

The late, great Robert Henry and his family—Marilyn, Brent and Patrick—for taking me under their wing to open doors I didn't know existed.

Mark Sanborn, who has been a great friend and mentor for the past several years.

Jim and Barbara Weems of Ad Graphics Inc., for their incredible patience with this "rookie" author.

My editors—Pam Mellskog, for your time, effort and meticulous care to make this book what it is and Lauren Gullion for creative direction.

My supporting cast of Dawn Chase, Gwen Postoak, Shari Williams, Terri Peterson, Kathy Bancroft, Kathy Campbell, Darius Smith and Dixie Dorman—you've been with me from "go."

April Lea Go Forth for lighting a fire of great expectations and then holding my feet to it.

Selo Black Crow, John Chaske, Melvin Gray Bear, Donnie and Alfreda Beartrack and my Sun Dance family for showing me a life-changing path.

The United States Air Force for investing in my growth in every way imaginable and allowing me to work with and lead the finest people I've ever met.

And to my friends and family who supported me.

Prologue

GRANDPA sat on the porch in his rocking chair with a Pendleton blanket draped over his shoulders. He watched the sun melting into the horizon behind the buildings and smiled. His grandson, Justin, was coming up the sidewalk and dusting himself off after another day of work at Jacob's Construction Company. He looked like a common laborer with his sinewy frame fitted into a flannel shirt, jeans and work boots. But his grandfather knew there was so much more to this young man.

Justin grew up in a town called Solitary, which bordered the state's largest Indian reservation. The only things the town had plenty of were poverty, unemployment and despair. He had tried college several years after high school, but soon dropped out.

At age twenty-seven, Justin's life was headed nowhere fast. On his Grandpa's invitation, he decided to move to the city of Sunlight to live with him. He figured his chances of getting steady work were much better here in Sunlight than back in his dead-end hometown.

Still, Justin often felt caught between two worlds. He was proud of his Native American heritage, but felt adrift in modern society. Every day he felt the pressure of trying to live and succeed in what he considered two distinctly different worlds. He deeply admired his grandfather for achieving success in both.

Grandpa pulled his white hair back into two neat braids and wore coveralls most of the time. The old man enjoyed a peaceful and happy life, spending his days with his grandchildren and friends in the community.

But before retiring, Grandpa taught high school and served on the Sunlight city council for many years. In this way, he helped bring many positive changes to his town. For this reason, many people—including Justin—respected and admired Grandpa as a leader. You see, the city of Sunlight used to be just a dead-end town too . . .

"Hi Grandpa," Justin mumbled with a troubled expression.

"What's the matter, Grandson?" Justin plopped down on the porch steps and dust rose off his clothes. He was silent for a moment, as if he couldn't find the words to speak.

"My life," Justin finally sighed with exasperation. "Everything seems so difficult, so confusing. I'm not sure how or why it all happened, but I'm lost, Grandpa. I feel empty inside." Justin shifted restlessly as he sat.

"Every day, I get up, go to work and come home dead tired. Then, I eat, go to bed and just do it all again. For what?"

Justin wanted an answer that Grandpa couldn't give him.

"I had such big dreams when I was a kid. My life is just a complete mess now. I moved to Sunlight because I thought it would be different from Solitary. It's a different location, but I've got the same problems."

Justin thrust his head into his hands as he sat on the wooden steps. Grandpa looked upon his grandson with a twinkle in his eye. He had been waiting for this chance for years. Grandpa had watched helplessly as Justin floundered in Solitary, refusing to accept support or advice from anyone. His heart ached to help Justin during that time. Instead, he waited patiently, believing that this very moment would arrive someday.

Now that it had, Grandpa felt an emotional mix of eagerness to show Justin a higher path and a desire to preserve the gravity of the moment. Grandpa cleared his throat and took a deep breath, hoping the Creator would guide his words and make this a night worth remembering—for Justin's sake.

"Justin," Grandpa said graciously, "let me tell you a story."

The Tiny Warrior

CHAPTER ONE

Cricket Tales

A LONG TIME AGO a village existed in a beautiful valley not far from where the city of Sunlight now stands. In that village lived a little Indian boy named Cricket. He lived with his mother and uncle since his father had taken ill and died near the time of Cricket's birth. Just eight years old, Cricket had already begun dreaming about becoming a great warrior for his people. But he was an unruly child. Cricket didn't know much about being a warrior and hoped someone would guide him on the path to his dream.

One day, a hunting party from a neighboring village paid a visit, and there was a feast to celebrate their arrival. A great warrior named War Club led the hunting party. Tribes across the land recognized him for his courage and feats in battle. Cricket would often sneak out at night to hear stories about him around the campfires.

When Cricket's Uncle Pipestone carried a gift of wrapped tobacco to the hunting party one night, Cricket followed close behind. Cricket considered this a perfect opportunity to see a mighty warrior up close. Before he knew it, Cricket was inside War Club's lodge. Uncle Pipestone gave War Club the tobacco and then looked down to see Cricket standing at his side.

"War Club, this is my nephew, Cricket," Pipestone said proudly. War Club nodded silently to Cricket, who was breathless and wide-eyed from seeing the warrior up close. Battle scars riddled War Club's brown skin, and he was as tall as a canoe. His arms were logs. His chest was a granite slab and his head a cooking pot. Cricket now understood why others revered War Club as one of the mightiest warriors in the land!

Cricket left the lodge and walked alone for a while, depressed. Meeting War Club only made his dream feel even more out of reach. After all, Cricket was often teased for being so small and skinny compared to other children his age. When a vivid image of War Club's mighty stature floated through his mind, he thought, "I'll never be a warrior."

Cricket eventually made it to the river and there spotted his uncle fishing on a rock.

❖   ❖   ❖

Justin grimaced at his Grandfather and rubbed his head.

"Grandpa, I know you're only trying to help me, but your stories are from another time. The world is different now—we have computers, jets, big cities. Everything moves at the speed of light. They're even talking about cloning a person, like they do in sci-fi movies!"

Grandpa sat unruffled with a warm glow in his eyes.

"Besides Grandpa, this is a children's story, and I'm not a child anymore."

"Oh, but you are, Justin, in so many ways," Grandpa quipped with a loving grin. "Come on, all you're going to do is go inside and watch TV. Spend some time with your old, white-haired grandpa." Grandpa held his hand over his heart and squinted, pretending to be on his deathbed. "What do you have to lose? Let's visit for a while."

Justin smiled in agreement.

CHAPTER ONE
Points of Wisdom

- Your capability in life should not be based on what others can do, but only on what you can do.

- The simplest lessons in life are often the most powerful. Truth requires few words.

- Times change, but true wisdom and the power of the human spirit are timeless classics.

- You may search long and hard for answers and powers you already possess.

- The child you were will always affect and be part of who you are.

- However long or far you go, you cannot outrun your life's problems when those problems are within.

Flow to Your Goals

WIIAT'S THE MATTER, Cricket?" Uncle Pipestone said, lowering his fishing net onto a nearby rock.

"Uncle, I know I'll never be a warrior. War Club is so big and strong, and I'm so little and weak. There is so much to learn, so much training to become a warrior. It all seems impossible," Cricket replied. Pipestone grinned as he looked up the river and recalled the challenges he had faced and conquered to become a warrior.

"Becoming a warrior does require much learning and training, but it's not impossible, Cricket. It will take persistence and patience," he explained. With wet hands Pipestone stroked his scalp lock, the long lock of ebony hair on his shaved head. He then pointed at the river.

"Your answers lie here, Cricket," he continued, admiring the flowing waters. Pipestone picked up his nets and waded out into the river. Cricket was confused, and he sat for a long time looking around for the answers to his questions. He became mesmerized watching the crystal waters swirl and bubble among the rocks.

When the sun started sinking below the birch-covered hillside, Pipestone packed his nets and the fish he'd caught. Donning his moccasins, he decided to help his nephew understand the lesson.

"What does water do when it comes to a rock, Nephew?" Pipestone asked. Cricket's face twisted with thought as he looked at the racing river current.

"It goes over it?" Cricket finally answered with a toothy smile.

"Right. It goes over it, or . . .?"

Cricket pondered carefully during the short silence.

"Around it!" Cricket exclaimed.

"Or?"

"Under it!"

"Yes, Nephew. And if the water cannot find any other way, with time and persistence the water will go through the rock one grain at a time. Once the water knows where it wants to go, it's unstoppable; it always finds a way to get there."

Pipestone picked up his gear and started walking. He looked back over his broad shoulder.

"Come on, Cricket, or we'll be late for dinner."

The mention of dinner made Cricket spring to his feet. He was starving! Cricket sprinted down the path ahead of Pipestone, and thoughts of dinner entered his mind with each step closer to home.

Cricket was unstoppable as he ran over the rocks, under logs, around the trees and through the branches. The lesson he learned made perfect sense as he threw open the flap to the lodge and smelled the thick aroma of boiling stew hanging in the air. Dinnertime at last!

✤　✤　✤

"Speaking of dinner . . ." Justin teased. "Good story, Grandpa, but I'm getting hungry. How about you?"

Grandpa retorted, "What is it you've always wanted to do with your life?" Justin looked out into the abyss of the sunset. After several minutes, he replied.

"I always wanted to be an engineer. I wanted to create designs and build them," Justin shared as he closed his eyes in pain and bowed his head. That foolish thought seemed more distant now than it ever had been. He tried to justify his disappointment.

"And I guess I'm close with this construction job. I help build things, right?" Justin felt as empty as the words sounded.

He wistfully remembered childhood days spent building things with Popsicle sticks, mud or whatever else was around. He was truly happy when he was creating things with his mind and hands. The construction job was a poor substitute for that dream, and he knew it.

"But why aren't you an engineer, Justin?" Grandpa asked, breaking the silence. Countless obstacles, setbacks and frustrations invaded Justin all at once. Tears welled up in his eyes, and he couldn't find the words or the voice to express them. He felt like a complete failure at that moment, unable to control even the single drop spilling from his left eye. It trailed down the side of his nose, over his lips and down his chin and neck to mix with the dust of his collar.

Humiliated, he reconsidered Grandpa's story about Cricket, the water and his life. He saw the connection. Life could have been so different. He could now see where he might have flowed instead of stopped. The newfound insight overwhelmed and embarrassed him. Hastily wiping his eyes, Justin rose.

"I was on the radial-arm saw today," Justin coughed. "I think I've got some wood dust in my eyes. I'm going to get a Coke, Grandpa. You want one?"

Grandpa declined the offer. He felt sadness stretching its wings inside of him as Justin walked into the house. Had he hit his grandson with too much truth at once and scared him away? Grandpa sat alone, holding his pipe and rubbing the stem anxiously, hoping he hadn't failed. Just then, Justin returned to the porch, popped the lid off the can and took a big swallow of the fizzing beverage.

"So, what happens to this Cricket guy next?" Justin asked as he plopped down onto the porch steps.

CHAPTER TWO
Points of Wisdom

- Whether you go under, over, around or through, find a way to flow to your goals.

- With persistence and patience, no undertaking is impossible to achieve.

- Settling for second best or good enough is neither the best nor enough for your life.

- Sometimes the answers you seek are hidden right out in the open.

- You will feel true joy when you align your talent and ability with your life path.

- Don't be afraid to see your life as it is—even if it's not what you want it to be. That is the first step toward positive change and fulfillment.

Keeping the Fire Lit

ONE NIGHT, Cricket couldn't sleep. Thunder rumbling in the distance kept him awake. So, he decided to sneak out of his lodge and look for adventure. Wandering toward the village fire, he noticed the outline of the firekeeper, Cloud Man, in front of the dancing tails of orange. Cloud Man looked nervous as Cricket approached.

"What's the matter, Cloud Man?" Cricket whispered.

"It's my wife, Cricket. We're about to have our first baby," Cloud Man replied with a grimace as he stared into the bright flames.

"Then why don't you go to your lodge?" Cricket asked.

"I'd like to, but I can't, Cricket. My responsibility is to the village as firekeeper. This fire represents the spirit of our people and must never go out—the village depends on it. I'll have to wait until morning." Just then, Cloud Man's sister came running up to him.

"Come quickly, your wife needs you," she said, wide-eyed. Cloud Man felt torn.

"I can watch the fire for you, Cloud Man," Cricket volunteered with an eager sparkle. "Go ahead! I can do it!"

After some debate, Cloud Man accepted Cricket's offer and hurried to the lodge where his wife labored.

Now, Cricket really felt like a grown-up. He sat near the fire, putting on the wood as Cloud Man had shown him before going to his wife. Cricket watched the fire dance and flicker. The warmth made him so comfortable that he soon fell asleep, even though he promised he wouldn't.

Early in the morning a group of angry hunters from his village nudged Cricket awake. They had been lost in fog on their way home from the hunt and had depended on the light of the village fire to guide them, but it wasn't there. The hunters looked dirty, hungry and tired. Cricket realized that one of them had even been injured. He felt horrible.

"I couldn't help it," Cricket stuttered. "The fire was so warm, and I was so tired. I just . . ."

The hunters slowly turned and walked away. Nothing Cricket said—no excuse—seemed to make him or the hunters feel better. He had broken his commitment to Cloud Man, the hunters and the village.

✤   ✤   ✤

"Gosh, I sure know how that feels." Justin explained. At his last job in Solitary he worked at a small store called Henry's Auto Parts. The owner, Mr. Henry, put great faith in Justin's ability. He grew to like and trust Justin.

At the time, Mr. Henry was working on a huge contract to provide parts to the fleet of the O'Connor Farms milk trucks. This contract would mean a great deal to the business and to Justin. Mr. Henry was going to give Justin a large raise to help him save money and go back to college.

"Everything was going my way, and I promised myself that I wouldn't blow it this time," Justin reflected. "Mr. Henry had to deliver some final paperwork for the deal and asked me to close the shop at the end of the day. At closing time my friends came by with concert tickets for that night. I was excited. In my hurry, I forgot to secure the back door and set the security alarm. In a way, I let the fire go out, just like Cricket."

The next day, Mr. Henry opened the shop and discovered the place had been robbed clean. His insurance only covered part of what he lost. So, literally overnight Mr. Henry found himself near financial ruin. The worst was that Mr. Henry could not fulfill his contract with the O'Connor fleet. It forced him to lay off several employees, and Justin was one of them.

"It seemed like a small thing to forget at the time, Grandpa," Justin confessed. "I had no idea it would have such an impact." Justin swallowed hard and scratched at a piece of tar on his boot.

"I should have secured that door! I promised him I would take care of his store, but I was more concerned about myself." The pain of the memory crashed in on Justin like relentless waves on a beach. "I guess I'm not cut out for responsibility."

"Now wait a minute, Justin," Grandpa interrupted, leaning forward in his chair. "That's only true if you make it that way. When other people depend on you, it's important to realize what can happen if you don't keep your commitments. But we all make mistakes, and there's no sense in focusing on them. We can only control where our life goes and what we do one day at a time. And every day we get a new chance to make the right decisions."

Grandpa leaned back into his chair and lit his pipe.

"Besides, Justin, it's never too late to keep a promise, especially to yourself." His words floated in the air with the pipe smoke.

Justin lifted his eyes and savored the first stars of the evening. The scattered points of light never seemed so sharp and luminescent. The two sat in silence for some time. Justin finally turned to his grandfather with clear eyes, having been released from his own prison of guilt. Grandpa took the cue and cleared his throat to continue.

CHAPTER THREE
Points of Wisdom

- Keep the fire lit by remembering this: No matter how good the excuse, it cannot justify a broken commitment.

- Mistakes happen. You must forgive yourself, learn the lessons and move on.

- The impact of your actions is often far-reaching and unknown. It may affect many others.

- You can only create and control your life path one day at a time.

- You will be rewarded and judged by actions, not intentions.

- It is never too late to keep a promise to yourself.

Find Your Own Way

STILL FEELING ASHAMED for letting the village fire go out, Cricket slunk off into the woods for solitude. He found a huge maple tree, rested his head on the roots and slowly began to cry. Only moments had passed when the old maple spoke.

"I can't live on the saltwater in your tears, little boy."

"You can talk?" asked the startled Cricket.

"Of course. Everything in nature has a voice if people will only listen. Now, why are you crying?"

"I'll never be a warrior," Cricket sobbed. "It's too hard. There's too much to it." The maple began to chuckle and Cricket felt frustration rising in him.

"What's so funny?" the sad little boy demanded. Cricket stood and adjusted his breechcloth.

"That I have no eyes and can see better than you!" the maple responded. "Through the years, I've endured wind, rain, drought, fire, snow, lightning and floods. It has twisted me. I've lost branches, and I've almost died many times. Still, I live. Through it all, I've become stronger. You see, those things are hard to survive, but I have a purpose in my life." The proud tree seemed to grow ten feet just mentioning this.

"I serve as a home to the squirrel family, the bird family and a bee colony." The massive maple pointed with the delicate tips of its branches as it spoke. "I provide sap for your people and shade so moss and mushrooms can grow. The more I think about my purpose, the deeper my roots grow. What is your purpose?"

"To be a warrior!" Cricket shouted after drying his tears with his arm.

"Why?" the maple inquired. Cricket was confused. He had never thought about that. The maple spoke one last time.

"You see, little boy, until you know your purpose, everything you do will be too hard."

Justin suddenly stood and walked to the other side of the porch. With scrunched eyebrows and a lowered gaze, the young man mouthed words to himself as he paced. Suddenly, he lit up with a question.

"Grandpa, do you know why I always wanted to be an engineer?"

Grandpa sat rocking in his chair and simply smiled. He knew the answer, but he hadn't heard it in many years.

"I wanted to build creative, wonderful things!" Justin exclaimed. "I wanted to build a youth facility with a pool, a park, a library and a climbing course."

Grandpa understood the desolation of Justin's home town of Solitary. Children there lacked parks and places to swim. Instead, they played in broken-down cars and garbage dumps. Even the library, a converted trailer filled mostly with discarded magazines and old copies of *Farmer's Almanac*, was grossly inadequate. Yet, as Justin continued, Grandpa could see something in him that he hadn't seen in years: the eyes of a child.

"I can see every detail, each color. I can see the children laughing, playing and learning. I've seen it a hundred times in my mind!" Justin explained, his mood suddenly shifting.

"That was a long time ago," the grandson acknowledged. "Life got so complicated! I was getting hit from every angle with suggestions about my career, school, where I should live, who I should call, what website to explore . . . Ah!" Justin ran his fingers through his hair and grabbed a tuft in each hand.

"I was following everyone's advice but my own. I got so overwhelmed that I finally just left it alone.

I knew the job I had wasn't taking me anywhere, but it seemed safe at the time." Justin looked deflated. "I don't know the moment I gave up on my dreams, but everything since then has been downhill."

Grandpa continued to rock in his chair. Then he reminded Justin that their people had always believed in visions.

"How do I know if it's a vision or just a wish, Grandpa?" Justin stammered.

"When you have a vision, you'll know," Grandpa said, lowering his voice. "It calls to you when you're quiet. It shows itself to you if you're still for a moment. Why do you think we isolate ourselves from everyone and everything, fasting and praying for four days at a time during a Vision Quest ceremony? It's like letting the dirt settle in a mud puddle so you can see clearly. And if you have a vision and don't follow it, you'll never be truly fulfilled. If you do follow it, there's no limit to your joy."

"I saw a T-shirt that said 'Live the life you love. Love the life you live.' I haven't done much of either so far, Grandpa," Justin said, looking up at the stars, now in full glory.

"Someday, you're gonna look like me, Justin," Grandpa promised, melodramatically squinting and wobbling his head. "Old and gray, sonny. So what are you waiting for?" Justin chuckled at his Grandpa's "old geezer" impression and flirted with the idea.

"Yeah, but do you know how old I'd be by the time I graduate if I went back to college?" the grandson asked.

"I sure do, Justin. You'd be exactly the same age you'd be if you didn't go." They both laughed out loud.

"Justin, our people moved over great distances with canoes. In those canoes, we carried everything—clothes, food, tools, sacred items. You name it. It was the first 'mobile home,' Justin." They both laughed again. "Our people went great distances like this, but they would have gone nowhere without the power of a magical item." Justin leaned forward to hear the answer.

"A paddle! Your life is in the canoe. But, just as you must drop your paddle into the water to reach your destination one stroke at a time, you do the same in life with your decisions and actions. Otherwise, you'll just float and go nowhere fast."

"That's what I've been doing, Grandpa. Just floating, floating in the wrong direction, too."

"Well, it's never too late in life to change direction, to paddle your canoe where you want it to go—toward that vision, Justin." Grandpa paused for a moment. "I know you mentioned dinner earlier."

"I'm OK, Grandpa," Justin quickly answered. "Tell me some more."

"Well, speaking of food, let me tell you this story."

CHAPTER FOUR
Points of Wisdom

- Find a thing to call your own. Once you know your purpose and pursue it, life changes from a frustrating struggle to an adventure.

- Knowing *what* you want to do with your life is vastly more important than *how* you get there.

- When you let the mud settle, you can see the bottom of the puddle clearly.

- Live the life you love. Love the life you live.

- Spend your time wisely for it will surely be spent. Start now.

- It's never too late to change your direction.

- Don't make the classic life error—mistaking contentment and security for true happiness.

- Your vision for your life can either haunt you or fulfill you to the depths of your spirit.

- Think of your life as a canoe and your decisions and actions as your paddle. You'll get where you're going one stroke at a time with the decisions and actions you make.

Sweet Temptation

CRICKET loved the maple syrup his people harvested each spring. He craved it all year and dreamed about the sweet, creamy taste when he was tucked away in his lodge on winter nights. Cricket's favorites were the handfuls of small nuggets of hardened maple syrup his mother would make for him if it was a good harvest.

While snooping around the camp one day, Cricket grew restless and hungry as he smelled the fires warming the golden sap. He ducked into his own family's lodge and there spotted a small clay jar full of cooling syrup!

Cricket just couldn't help himself. Quick as a wink, he snatched the jar and dashed away to the river and greedily plunged his fingers into the succulent syrup. Though not quite as tasty as the nuggets, he gorged himself like a hungry wolf anyway. It was too good to resist!

Before long, when the jar was nearly empty, Cricket felt he would die as his stomach churned the rich nectar. But he wasn't too sick to fear punishment. So, he threw the jar into the river to hide the evidence. Then he stumbled home, holding his stomach and moaning in pain.

When his mother noticed him approaching the lodge, she led him in to lie down.

"My poor Cricket must be getting sick. I'll make you some tea," she gently murmured. She began gathering what she needed when Cricket's uncle walked in and whispered hurriedly to her. As quickly as he came in, he left. Cricket's mother still stood there with a heart-broken expression.

"I have some bad news, Cricket. Your uncle had permission from the chief to set aside a jar of syrup for you so I could make your favorite, maple nuggets." Cricket's mother fought to hold back her tears of disappointment. "But someone has stolen the jar."

Cricket wanted to explain what had happened, but he couldn't talk due to the agony of his stomach.

"We're so sorry, Cricket," his mother said with regret. But it was Cricket who was truly sorry!

Justin took a deep breath and eyed the crescent moon high above while he contemplated Grandpa's words.

"Grandpa, I never told you about a chance I had that would have made a huge difference in my life," he finally shared.

"What happened, Justin?" Grandpa inquired.

"Remember about five years ago, when I was working construction on the new clinic over in Granite City?"

Grandpa nodded.

"Quest Engineering was the firm that designed it. One of their project managers, Brian Lawson, came out for a site visit. We'd had a bunch of delays, and he wanted to know why."

Justin described meeting with his team to remedy the delays. One major problem on the project involved the company's use of brace fittings with the wrong specifications.

"Those things weren't going to hold the load being placed on them," Justin recalled. "Instead of spending a little more money to order new fittings, the workers were just trying to force them into place. That took more time and would have caused problems that needed to be fixed later. I brought the issue up and got a nasty glare from my foreman. After the meeting, Mr. Lawson came up to me and told me how impressed he was with my courage to speak up and my knowledge about construction and design." Justin beamed, remembering the moment.

"He encouraged me to apply for an internship with Quest Engineering. Mr. Lawson said Quest often helped interns pay for college, too. The internship paid peanuts, but he said the program would teach me about the engineering business. Mr. Lawson told me to think of it as an investment in myself." Justin then kneaded his forehead.

"I got the application, and it was thick! I started filling it out, but never finished," Justin said and looked away in embarrassment. "Plus, I was making so much more money doing construction. I couldn't see giving that up for three months. I was comfortable where I was without all the hassles I would have . . ." Justin stopped suddenly. He knew he was justifying his poor decision now just as he had then.

"Gosh, I'm such an idiot! I actually thought I was getting away with something by not filling out the application. I'd probably have more free time *now,* more money *now,* had I just filled out the paperwork." Justin bit his lip in regret. "I needed that internship, Grandpa."

"No, Justin, you didn't *need* it. You only *wanted* it. There's a huge difference," Grandpa declared. "Justin, there will always be temptations and distractions in life but when we feel we truly need something, we find a way to get it. In the old days, our people would concentrate all their efforts, skills and drive toward hunting because they *needed* food.

"If you truly *needed* that internship, you would have found a way to do whatever it took to get it. You need to understand the difference between *wants* and *needs* because that's where temptation in life can get the best of you."

Justin rubbed his chin and pondered. "I guess at the time I only wanted it, but I realize now that I needed it. I knew the guy who got the internship," he continued. "Last year, I heard he was already an assistant project manager on a beautiful new museum and making four times the amount I was making at construction! Man, did he get lucky." Grandpa adjusted his woolen blanket.

"Justin, what's done is done, but luck had nothing to do with it," the old man stated flatly. "The things you do today always make an impact and will affect where you end up tomorrow. Getting what you need sometimes requires great sacrifice and time, but those are the things that will truly fulfill you and make such a difference in the end.

"You can grab a green apple off the tree in the front yard today and have the problems that Cricket had. Or you can be patient, focused and bent on going one day at a time. That way, you'll eventually get a sweet red apple. To do it any other way is like planting corn and expecting coconuts to appear." Justin attempted to smile.

"I see what you mean," Justin conceded. "I thought I was getting ahead at the time. But it ended up being a huge loss in the long run." Then he stood up and walked toward the screen door. "I'm gonna make a PB and J sandwich. You want one, Grandpa?"

"Sure, Justin. That'd be fine," Grandpa said with a nod. A few minutes later, Justin came out with two sandwiches and some napkins. The two sat on the porch, commenting on the bread and the jelly quality. But Justin was most hungry for the wisdom his Grandpa was serving. So, they soon wiped their mouths and got back to the real meal of the evening.

CHAPTER FIVE
Points of Wisdom

- Life is full of sweet temptations. Don't seize a short-term gain if long-term pain is a consequence.

- Know the difference between wants and needs. You'll find a way to get what you feel you truly need if you don't allow yourself to be distracted by all your wants.

- Don't plant corn seed and expect coconuts. The quality, level of achievement and joy of your life balances with what you put into it.

- Understand that others may see talent and ability you don't see or appreciate in yourself.

- Your fear of success can sometimes be even stronger than your fear of failure.

- Discipline is the technique of harnessing your own incredible power to move you forward.

- Success is choosing your sacrifices. Consider the time, energy and effort you use to improve yourself as an investment.

- Choices today will determine where you'll be tomorrow.

CHAPTER SIX

Choose Your Pack

CRICKET was once again alone in the forest, this time searching for blueberries. As he popped into a clearing, he saw a group of coyotes chase a rabbit into its hole. The coyotes stood in a circle around the rabbit hole, knowing that was the end of the chase.

Cricket could see, even from a distance, this bunch had what he wanted—a group of friends. Although he knew the coyotes were tricksters, that knowledge only added to his curiosity and excitement. The coyote leader, Backbone, soon noticed Cricket moving closer.

"Little boy, can you reach down this hole and grab the rabbit?" he slyly asked. Cricket felt important and needed, but he didn't want the coyotes to know.

"Why should I help you?" the boy snorted and proudly stroked his unkempt hair. Backbone was a trickster, and he was no fool. He could see in Cricket's eyes the desire to be a part of the group. Backbone smiled grimly.

"We'll let you play with us. You can be a coyote, too." Cricket quickly agreed, reached down the hole and pulled out the rabbit. In a blink of an eye, the hungry pack of coyotes gobbled the furry creature.

After that, Cricket ran with the coyotes for many days. He played where they played, ate what they ate and learned how to yip, bark and howl.

When he returned to his village, he acted strangely. He began biting and scratching his skin. He lied to his mother and even stole some blueberries from his neighbor. Cricket was becoming a trickster, too!

"What has gotten into you lately?" Uncle Pipestone asked. Cricket howled and barked and ran off to be with his coyote friends.

Eventually though, the boy noticed that while he was always tired, the coyotes were getting fat and lazy. No wonder. Cricket was doing all the work for them—picking berries, pulling rabbits from their holes and climbing trees to catch squirrels. One day, the coyotes had an appetite for fish.

"Fish is our favorite," Backbone explained, "but we hardly catch any. We usually must wait until a fisherman or a bear leaves scraps." Backbone soon convinced Cricket to follow his plan to get some delicious fish for the pack.

Cricket carefully stepped on each rock until he got to

a place where he could spear the fish as they swam. He had seen his uncle do this a hundred times and thought it couldn't be *that* difficult. Cricket waited patiently for a fish, but the coyotes grew restless.

"Hurry up, little boy! You're taking too long, and we're hungry!" the coyotes howled.

Cricket felt the pressure and lost his focus. He slipped on a mossy rock and plunged into the river's icy waters.

"Help me!" Cricket screamed and begged as he began floating away. "Please, my coyote brothers—do something!"

Backbone and the other coyotes yipped and howled at the sudden entertainment as they ran along the riverbank to watch the rapids whisk Cricket away.

✠   ✠   ✠

"Wow, does that story hit home!" Justin fumed. His fist clenched, he explained how his so-called friends had shaped and molded his behavior.

"Remember the two guys I hung around with in high school? Chuck and Stan?" Justin trailed off. Grandpa knew exactly who he was talking about due to the many troubled phone calls he had received from Justin's parents many years earlier. Justin was an honors student in high school, and he displayed great talent at a young age. However, Chuck and Stan's charisma appealed to him. They were headed nowhere fast, but the ride looked like fun at the time.

The problem was, the more time Justin spent with Chuck and Stan, the more he had to do to please them. Those guys made a convenient habit of copying Justin's homework, using him to do their school projects and even pushing Justin to cover for them when they skipped school.

No teacher ever suspected Justin would lie about these things, but he did. The more time he spent around Chuck and Stan, the more he neglected his dreams of college and a career in engineering.

"I desperately wanted to be accepted by those guys and was willing to pay any cost," Justin admitted. "I was tired of being 'Dudley Do Right' all the time. It was like being so thirsty that you'd be willing to drink saltwater. But the more I got, the more I needed until my dreams shriveled. Neither of them would have passed high school without me!" The truth was being revealed, and it stung.

"It didn't end with high school. Those guys talked me into waiting to go to college," Justin added, shaking his head. He mocked Chuck's voice: "Why ruin the next couple years with more school?" Justin bit the inside of his cheek.

"I settled for doing whatever Chuck and Stan wanted to do. But those guys never gave a damn about me!"

Grandpa sensed Justin's pain and put his hand on his grandson's shoulder.

"The spirit works like a sponge, and it will absorb whatever and whoever it happens to be around. It is up to us to choose the things for it to soak up."

Justin proceeded to tell Grandpa that Chuck and Stan moved away to get work in other towns a couple years later. But by then, he was stuck in Solitary working odd jobs. Justin's face bore a cynical, forced smile.

"You know what the kicker was? For the first time, I asked them for help. I asked if I could stay with them for a few days to interview for jobs, and if they would put in a good word for me at their workplaces. Neither happened," Justin growled as he pounded his fist into his other hand.

"I allowed myself to be defined by those jerks. I asked for their approval on everything. I didn't appreciate my own worth or talent—and I had so much."

"What do you mean, *had*?" Grandpa shot back and then smiled warmly at Justin. "Do you know that when baby eagles learn to fly, their parents literally lift them up if they're falling? They fly under the fledgling and give it a boost, helping it go higher. Those are the kind of people you need to surround yourself with in life, the ones that help you fly, not the ones that give you reasons to stay on the ground." Grandpa pulled out a pouch of tobacco to refill his pipe.

CHAPTER SIX
Points of Wisdom

- Choose your pack wisely. Your spirit is like a sponge, soaking up who and what surrounds it.

- If you suspect that you are being used, you probably are.

- In true friendship, you are never required to surrender your character or your dreams for approval.

- Don't allow others to define who you are or what you're capable of. That is your responsibility.

- Follow your heart and make the choices that are right for you. Only you will truly know what those are.

- Surround yourself with positive people and influences that help you fly—not those that give you reasons to stay on the ground.

Cast Your Reflection

CRICKET, watch out!" But it was too late. In an instant, Cricket had dropped his uncle's best fishing spear into the swiftly moving river. Pipestone fumed, thinking of the amount of time that he had spent creating the masterpiece. "This morning you tipped over a whole basket of corn and nearly burned the lodge down, and now you've dropped my best spear after I told you not to touch it. What has gotten into you today?"

"I don't know, Uncle," Cricket replied meekly.

"Well, I think you need to spend some time finding the answer," Pipestone groused.

Cricket took his uncle's advice and walked along his favorite trail to think about the reasons he acted the way he did. He swam in his favorite part of the river and took a nap under his favorite tree. But, at the end of the day, he had no answers. The next morning, Cricket greeted his uncle and told him of his problem.

"Uncle, I still don't know why I act the way I do sometimes," Cricket confessed. Pipestone's eyes sparkled.

"Don't worry, Cricket. I discovered who is to blame for all your misbehaving."

"Really, Uncle?" Cricket felt better already, knowing he wasn't the reason. "Who is it?" Cricket asked.

"He lives in Blue Pond. When you peer over the edge you'll see the one to blame, and you can ask him to stop getting you into trouble. But watch out! He's an ugly little cuss and can be rowdy. Be cautious."

Cricket headed to Blue Pond. A bit nervous, he chewed on a piece of sage and tried to enjoy the perfect day. When he arrived, he got on his belly and crawled to the bank. Just as his uncle had told him, Cricket slowly peered over the edge.

He could see a head emerging. It had a tuft of wild hair, small ears and two big eyes. It had a button nose and rounded cheeks. Why, it was Cricket! When he smiled, the lake smiled. When he laughed, the lake laughed with him. But, when he scowled and stuck his tongue out, the lake returned the insult.

Cricket sat there for quite some time and heard his mother's voice: "When you arise in the morning to greet the sun, do so with joy in your heart and the world will return it."

Cricket felt the warmth of the sun on his back as he

walked back to the village. He showed up just in time to see the chief sharing stories and lessons with the children. The chief was a stocky man with kind eyes and a wide smile. He was intent on telling his story.

"In my right hand, I have the tiny invisible spirit of a dog. He is cruel, vicious and mean," the chief began. "In my left hand, I have the tiny invisible spirit of another dog. This one is loyal, friendly and kind. Each day when I wake up, the two tiny spirits fight with each other."

Cricket hung on every word and couldn't wait for the ending.

"Which one wins?" Cricket asked in a rush. The chief seemed to beam at Cricket's curiosity.

"Whichever one I feed that day," the chief said with a broad grin. "We choose the reflection our spirit will cast to the world."

Deep in thought, Justin rolled a lock of his ebony hair between his fingers.

"Remember the youth facility and park I was telling you about?" Grandpa nodded.

"Sally Rusted Knife was on Solitary's city council and asked me to be a part of the planning committee to actually build it last year. She said my 'passion and ideas would be helpful.'" Justin chuckled sarcastically.

"But working with that group was impossible! Budgets, timelines, zoning issues, blah, blah, blah." Justin rocked his head back and forth.

"But Justin, that's all part of any city project. And this one was pretty important to you, wasn't it?"

Justin grunted.

"Heck yeah, but they got me so frustrated! And their attitudes—they were so nonchalant about it, like it didn't matter anyway. Like the chief said in the story, they were feeding that negative dog."

"Maybe that's why Sally wanted you on the planning committee," Grandpa said. "Perhaps she thought your passion and joy about the idea would build theirs as well."

"But when I brought up an idea, they would change it. Why should I be the one to always bend? I got into some nasty arguments with some of those hardheads . . ." Justin's faraway expression suddenly turned thoughtful. "Eventually I quit the committee. And you know, they never did build that youth facility and park."

Justin turned to Grandpa and said he understood the story about Cricket, Blue Pond and the importance of a good attitude.

"But man, they ruined that project!"

"You're close, Justin," Grandpa replied, grateful for Justin's attempt. "We control only one thing in this world, not nature, weather or other people. We can only control what we do. Cricket saw this when he looked over the ledge at his reflection, remember?" Justin nodded.

"Cricket smiled and the pond smiled. Cricket stuck out his tongue and the pond did likewise. That's the way the world works, too," Grandpa explained. "It will simply cast back the reflection you show it *first*." Justin swallowed hard, understanding his mistake.

"You mean I should have made the effort to get them to see the project through my eyes instead of arguing with them?"

Grandpa grinned mischievously.

"Well, I believe Sally asked you to be a part of that group because she thought your 'passion and ideas' would lead people to work together better, not to have better arguments." Grandpa got up and headed into the house. He returned with a small dented toolbox with a tiny lock.

"Justin, I want to show you something. But you have to open this locked toolbox to see it. I have the key in my hand and I'll give you five minutes to get that sucker open using anything on this porch." Justin felt a bit confused, but he still wanted to see the toolbox's contents. So, he pulled on the lock, banged it on the porch and tried prying it open with his house keys.

"There's no way I'll get that thing open without the key, Grandpa!"

"Then why didn't you ask me for it, Justin?"

Justin smiled at his obvious blunder.

"OK, you got me. So what's in the box?" Grandpa used a brass key to open the lock.

"Something very special and very valuable is right here in front of you," Grandpa said while lifting the lid. The toolbox was empty. Justin felt really confused now.

"Well, what the heck is that? Air?"

"Wisdom," Grandpa replied, glowing. "You can inspire and lead people to your ideas, ask for their help and help them understand your thoughts. Or, you can force the issue and turn them away. Did you ever honestly try to get the other committee members to see things through your eyes before you judged them to be 'hardheads'?"

"I can see your point," Justin said, deflated. He slowly realized the positive impact he might have had on the group.

"Justin, when it comes to your attitude and the reflection you cast to the world, you'll learn what Cricket learned looking in the water and the chief taught with the story of the dogs. You can be your own worst enemy or your best ally. But always remember, it is a choice only you can make for yourself."

CHAPTER SEVEN
Points of Wisdom

- ◼ Cast your reflection with purpose. The world works like a mirror. It will reflect what you give to it *first*.

- ◼ You can be your own worst enemy or best ally with the attitudes and behaviors you choose each day.

- ◼ Lead people to your ideas with kindness.

- ◼ Allow your passion and joy about an idea to help guide you through the effort it takes to make it materialize.

- ◼ The positive and negative "spirit dogs" fight for your attitudes every day. The one you feed determines the winner.

- ◼ The only thing you control in this world is what you do.

- ◼ The sooner you stop making excuses, the sooner you'll begin to make true progress toward your dreams.

A Bigger Lake,
a Better You

C RICKET sat by the banks of Crimson Lake and threw stones into the calm waters. As he tossed each pebble, he thought about the difficulties of growing up and trying to become a warrior. It all discouraged him greatly. He picked up another rock and flipped it.

"OUCH!" Cricket leaned over the edge of the bank and glimpsed a large salmon swimming in quick circles. "Watch where you're throwing those next time! What are you doing out here by yourself—are you fishing?" The salmon was nervous.

"No, just thinking. I want to be a warrior, but I have many things, impossible things, to do. I'm not sure anyone can understand, but I get afraid of what's ahead," Cricket sighed.

"Ah yes, yes, I see," the salmon said and then began mumbling to himself as if in deep thought. Cricket's eyes opened wider as he waited for some wisdom from the fish's lips.

"I didn't always live in Crimson Lake," the fish began. "I used to live many miles from here in a small watering hole connected to a river. Lots of other fish sped by my home, and I could hear them talking about a waterfall downriver. But I never followed them. Being such a small fish, I was afraid. One day, I moved to the edge of my water hole to get a closer look, and the current from the river grabbed me."

"Were you scared?" Cricket asked expectantly.

"Of course! But, it was a thrill to swim so fast. Plus, I wasn't alone. Everywhere there were salmon like me in the water. Then, I could see where the water ended and the falls began. And before I knew it, I was flying through the air and landing with a splash in Blue Pond." The salmon explained that his arrival at Blue Pond was a glorious experience for many reasons.

"Making the move was scary at first, but I found at Blue Pond something I never had before—friends that were like me. And you know what?"

"Tell me, tell me," Cricket blurted.

"I grew! I wasn't a small fry for long in Blue Pond. I was able to move around and explore new areas. I had new bugs to eat and new fish to talk with. It created a new me!"

Cricket looked puzzled.

"But how did you get all the way to Crimson Lake?" The salmon smiled and jumped high into the air.

"Like this! I kept finding new rivers that led to new lakes, and each time I learned more, grew more and got stronger for the next swim. Eventually, I'll make it to the ocean, just by going one lake at a time!"

✤ ✤ ✤

"Man, that salmon was on his way!" Justin cheered. "I understand just how he felt. I've lost count of how many times I didn't walk through a door that opened for me." Justin's heart was pounding as he viewed his life with fresh eyes. "So many times, I've settled for 'good enough' or second best. I see that now."

Grandpa's face was highlighted for a moment from the glow of his lit pipe.

"That internship with Quest Engineering could have been my ticket," Justin continued. "Mr. Lawson said he started the same way. I would've learned all about the engineering business—how to use design software and to run some of the meetings. Yet, I said I'd think about it." Justin had a distant look as if he were watching it happen all over again. "I went home and started to think of all the reasons why I'd be horrible at doing those things. I thought about . . . I just didn't want to fail and look stupid in front of the other guys, Grandpa. I mean, I wasn't even qualified for a position like that."

"Well, Mr. Lawson seemed to think you were," Grandpa said with confidence. "Sometimes you need to trust the belief others place in you until yours catches up." Grandpa put his hand on Justin's shoulder. "The most challenging thing you can do is break through the boundaries you set for yourself." Justin turned to look at Grandpa.

"My neighbor had a dog and got one of those fancy electronic collars. You know the kind that will shock 'em if they leave the yard? I sat out here and watched that dog getting zapped as he tried to leave the front yard. After a while, he knew what his boundary was and stopped trying."

Justin looked over at the neighbor's yard. "I guess hearing 'No' and 'You can't' all those times did the same thing to me."

"Now, look in our yard. You see that oak tree, Justin?" Grandpa asked. Justin nodded. "That big old tree started off as a little acorn the size of your thumbnail. Under the right conditions of light, water and soil, it's become that. And it's still growing."

"And people need the same thing, like you were saying earlier about baby eagles?" Justin shyly added.

"Exactly, Justin! We need to surround ourselves with the right people, ideas, and attitudes—the right conditions," Grandpa answered. Justin thought it all seemed to click so easily, too easily. He shook his head as if coming out of a daze.

"Yeah, but people are different than dogs or trees, Grandpa." Justin felt he should earn some credit for seeing the analogy's flaw.

"You're absolutely right, Justin. Unlike a dog, we know we can go anywhere we want to because the pain of leaving the yard is only temporary. And unlike an oak tree, we can *create* the right conditions and there's no limit to how large a person's mind or spirit can grow."

Grandpa gave Justin's shoulder a pat and began rocking in his chair.

CHAPTER EIGHT
Points of Wisdom

- A bigger lake, a better you. Change is often scary, but this is where your greatest growth will take place.

- Sometimes you must trust the belief others place in you until yours catches up.

- The most challenging thing involves breaking the boundaries you've set for yourself.

- You only gain courage *after* you take a risk.

- If the passion and desire for your dream outweighs your fears of looking foolish or failing, you will succeed.

- Under the right conditions, a tiny acorn will become a massive oak. People can create their own conditions and grow infinitely.

- Be a cheerleader, an enthusiastic believer in yourself and your dreams. Don't ever criticize yourself—there are critics who will do that for you.

- Don't allow the negative comments of others deter you; they are words that mean nothing unless you believe them.

CHAPTER NINE

We're All Connected

IN THE VILLAGE, Cricket was playing lacrosse with
the other children. He was faster than the other boys,
but because of his small size, he had difficulty handling
the long stick and kept tripping on it as he ran. Never-
theless, an older boy named Chasing Fox was jealous
of Cricket's speed and teased him for his clumsiness
with the stick. The chorus of laughter from the others
soon proved too much for Cricket to bear. Heartbroken,
he dropped his stick and left the game with tears in his
eyes.

Cricket wandered over to his Aunt Daisy's fire, which
was near the lacrosse grounds. He watched her scraping
hides and sewing moccasins. Cricket admired her con-
centration and her attention to detail as he watched
her transform the sheets of leather into footwear. Daisy

was making them for the hunting party preparing to depart. Busy as she was, she still noticed what had happened to Cricket on the lacrosse grounds as she worked.

"You know, Cricket," she began, "true power lies in your heart, not in your height." She smiled and continued to work.

"Then how come I'm the one always being pushed around?" Cricket grumbled. His eyes looked downcast as he twisted his moccasin in the dirt. "Cricket's clumsy. Cricket can't play. Cricket's too small," he said, imitating the jeers. "Who would notice or care if I just disappeared?"

Exasperated, Aunt Daisy firmly set her scraper down.

"Cricket, what is the most valuable thing in this village?" she demanded. Cricket thought hard for a moment and answered.

"Our shelter, because it keeps us dry and warm," he said confidently.

"No," Aunt Daisy replied. Cricket felt less and less sure of his answer.

"Our food, to keep us strong and healthy?" he guessed.

"No," Daisy said as her eyes seemed to look into his soul.

"Our, our wood for the fires to keep us warm," he muttered.

"No," Daisy impatiently answered. "Our most valuable thing in this village is each person. We need every single person to help the village survive each year, Cricket." Daisy smiled warmly now.

"Well, what can I do?" Cricket challenged. Daisy returned to the moccasins.

"I don't know. What *can* you do?" she teased. Just then, she paused and suddenly her whole body seemed struck with a painful expression.

"What's wrong, Aunt Daisy?" Cricket exclaimed. Daisy clutched her back and winced.

"It's my back, Cricket. Our medicine man, Black Fish, has my remedy but he's on the other side of the valley picking berries. Now I won't get these moccasins finished in time for the big hunt." Daisy lay on the ground in agony.

Cricket looked around, desperately hoping the answer would fall from the sky, but he knew it rested with him. In a flash, he disappeared through the thicket and moved as fast as his feet would carry him, darting and sprinting like a rabbit through the forest. He finally reached Black Fish and got a piece of root to help his Aunt Daisy.

"Oh my, Cricket. That was fast!" she announced when he returned. Cricket panted as he approached and offered her a small auburn root. Daisy chewed what Cricket handed her and immediately began feeling better. A grateful smile soon replaced the tension in her face.

"Do you know why we grow beans, corn and squash together, Cricket?" Aunt Daisy asked after the remedy took effect. Cricket gave her a blank look and a shrug. "We call them the 'three sisters' because they help each other stay strong and healthy."

Daisy walked Cricket out to the garden to show him how the vine of the bean wraps around the tall cornstalks. She also pointed out the squash and its large leaves spread close to the ground to keep the ground moist. Together, the tangled plants formed a barrier to prevent weeds from growing as well.

"Just as the three sisters work together, each villager needs to do the same. Just as you've helped me, I'm helping the hunters stay safe. And they provide food for us both. You see, Cricket, we all need to use the abilities the Creator gave us to support each other. We can only survive and prosper in that way. What happens to one affects the other. We're all connected. None of us grows alone, Cricket."

Justin was shaking his head and smiling. The story's lessons were making sense now. Consequently, he felt like the victim of life's practical joke, embarrassed that he'd been so naïve about the true cause of his problems.

"I wonder what Solitary would be like now if that youth facility and park *had* been built. I think part of the reason I was so hostile at those meetings was . . . Grandpa, I didn't understand half of what they were talking about! Zoning, bids, fund-raising—I was clueless." Grandpa raised his eyebrows at Justin, encouraging him to finish his thought.

"I know I should have asked for help, but I was too proud to show my ignorance; I didn't want to look weak," Justin confessed as he stared at his rugged boots. "I got defensive and pushed everyone away, from me *and* the project." Justin's shoulders slumped under the truth of the moment.

"If only I could have better understood the process, and they could have better understood my vision—why it was so important!" Justin stopped short. His perfect hindsight now seemed pointless. Justin took a deep breath and watched the red strobe of an airplane pass overhead.

"It wasn't the board that killed the project; it was me," Justin stated bluntly. The words hit him like a hammer, but smashed a burden he had carried since he abandoned the project.

"We could have had a great town, like Sunlight," Justin mused. "I look at all the things you did around here, Grandpa, and I think about what I could have done there . . ."

"Whoa now, Justin," Grandpa interjected. He rose from his rocker and stood at the edge of the porch to look out at the lights of the town. "This place used to be in bad shape, too. We were just like Solitary, but it wasn't me who changed it. It was the whole town working together."

"A bird and his mate can build a nest, but a colony of bees can build a whole hive and ants can build a city. That's what we did here with each one playing his part. Every person has power to do amazing and wonderful things. Now imagine what a few, a dozen or a community working together can do!" Grandpa's eyes blazed with passion as he remembered Sunlight's past community accomplishments.

"Like a jigsaw puzzle, everyone holds an important piece; you just have to find out what yours is, Justin. Combine that with others and you'll make some beautiful creations—that is what we did here." Grandpa looked deep into Justin's eyes.

"There's only one condition," Grandpa added, pausing to make his point. "You can't be concerned with who is going to get the credit. Justin, our success in life will be a direct balance with how much we help others achieve it. Like Daisy said, we're all connected in this way." Grandpa winked at Justin and pulled a long draw from his pipe.

CHAPTER NINE
Points of Wisdom

- You are connected in so many ways to so many others. No one grows alone.

- True power lies in your heart, not in your height.

- The most valuable asset to any group is the individual. Everyone has reservoirs of talent and ability that often go untapped.

- The "three sisters" show that though different from others, you are capable of making incredible contributions to a group's success.

- Each person has power to do amazing and wonderful things. Now imagine what a few, a dozen or a community working together can do.

- Like a jigsaw puzzle, everyone holds an important piece of the big picture. Find out what yours is.

- There is no limit to what a group can do when egos don't interfere.

- Your success in life will be a direct balance with how much you help others achieve it.

The Tiny Warrior

THUNDER exploded and shook the lodges, and a waterfall of rain poured from the sky. Cricket crouched next to his mother by the fire and listened uneasily to the wind's eerie sound whistling through camp. He had never experienced a violent storm like this. Then, to make matters worse, Cricket heard the distant voice of his Uncle Pipestone, yelling: "A flood is coming! Crimson Lake is overflowing!"

Cricket's mother sprang up and tried to gather their belongings. However, when Pipestone plunged into the lodge dripping and panting, he explained that they had no time. The river was already snaking into camp.

Cricket and his family dashed out into the chilly rain and met other villagers scurrying for higher ground. They were scaling the steep sides of the valley to find shelter among the rocks. Cricket glanced back and glimpsed the river knocking over lodge after lodge. Smoke mixed with rain as the water doused the campfires.

Over the storm's terrible sounds, Cricket heard the villagers crying. Planting season had begun and the people watched their cornfields wash away along with their lodges and belongings.

The chief talked rapidly to a group of men. He broke the painful news that the seed was gone, which made replanting impossible. The men all looked back at what used to be the village.

"Wait! Part of my lodge is still standing and there is a bag of seed," Pipestone shouted. Then, he and Cloud Man bolted down to brave the swift water and crashing trees. The whole village watched as the two scrambled to the lodge and tried to retrieve the bag that would give life back to the village. Pipestone used hand signals to tell the chief they could see it, but too many timbers lay across the lodge. They couldn't get inside.

From the high ground, the chief viewed a new surge coming down the valley from the lake. Trees and boulders bobbed within the swirling cauldron of debris. The chief frantically signaled with his arms for their return before the flood swept them away, too.

Cricket knew his people were in danger. With the seed gone, they wouldn't have enough food to make it through the winter. He also remembered all he had recently learned. Then, though afraid, he ran. Cricket ran like the wind of the storm that day, ducking falling branches and jumping from boulder to fallen tree until he reached the two warriors. Before they could stop him, Cricket had scrambled into the narrow entrance, grabbed the leather pouch of seed and popped out again.

Without a word, the three of them took off, leaping and bounding over obstacles and the water's deadly current. The other villagers held their breath as they watched swells of muddy water churning down the valley.

Cricket, Pipestone and Cloud Man reached higher ground just as the whirlwind of debris and water crashed into the village and filled the valley. Exhausted and breathless, Cricket collapsed onto the ground. The villagers gathered around to tend to him as he struggled to pull the pouch from his waist and weakly held it out to the chief. The chief opened the bag and looked up with elation.

"IT'S CORN!" he shouted. The village exploded with cheers for Cricket and the men.

When the storm ended and the water receded, the people of Cricket's village rebuilt their homes and re-planted their fields. Cricket worked as hard as anyone to make that happen. Then, the people held a huge feast to celebrate their achievement and give thanks. The drums stopped when the chief, bathed in the firelight, rose to speak.

"Tonight we give thanks to the Creator for all his blessings and for giving us the strength to rebuild our village. We also want to thank the Creator for a special gift in the form of a little boy named Cricket." Cricket could feel his heart stop at this unexpected turn of events. "Cricket, please step forward."

The village buzzed with joyful conversation and drums thundered in applause. Cricket barely came up to the chief's hip. The chief smiled warmly at Cricket and then spoke. "This boy saved our village. When we needed him most, he was there. He didn't think of himself, of the risk or the danger, but only of the survival of our people.

"A piece of ordinary flint is shaped and chipped into a sharpened arrowhead, a thing that has purpose and serves its maker," the chief continued. "Cricket is a boy whose spirit has been shaped and chipped. He understands the true meaning of what it is to be a warrior. A warrior's power does not lay in his strength, his size or feats in battle. A warrior's power lays in his heart, his character and his commitment to those whom he serves and protects."

The chief reached down and tied a beautiful eagle feather in Cricket's hair as the drummers sang an honor song to praise him for his deed. Cricket was happier than he could ever remember in his whole life—and just as surprised. His tiny size had always felt like a curse, but it proved priceless because it was one thing that had enabled him to save the village.

As he looked around, he saw that War Club and his band had arrived with their children, wives and elders. Cricket greatly admired War Club, but he now saw him in a different light. And he now understood what made him such a powerful warrior. With a nod and a smile, War Club gave his approval and respect to Cricket.

The days would pass as they always do. But not too many would go by before another band of visitors would come to the village. They would come great distances to pay respect and honor the great warrior who saved his people. When they saw Cricket, they were surprised he was only a boy. But the chief would tell Cricket's story and the visitors would play an honor song for Cricket. As the visitors looked at the little boy with his eagle feather fluttering in his hair, they saw the beauty of what people can become in this world. They saw the tiny warrior that lives inside us all.

Justin looked skyward at the bright stars and the vastness of space. He felt small. Yet, he felt more powerful than ever. He felt an energy waking and stirring inside of him, and he knew that he desperately needed guidance on this last point.

"Grandpa? Cricket saved his village and became a warrior by using his speed and his size. Nowadays, those things don't count for much," he noted. Grandpa knew where Justin was going.

"You were absolutely right earlier, Justin. The world *is* different now, but we're still in dire need of warriors. A warrior's purpose involved developing himself to become an asset to the village he served and protected.

"Today, that 'village' can be your family, your community, people at your school campus, clients, co-workers—anyone you serve. A warrior constantly asks, 'What am I doing to develop myself to better care for the people I serve?'" Justin's eyes lit up as he began to make the connection to his own life.

"And Justin, since the world is different now," Grandpa continued, "the training to become a warrior has changed too. No longer do warriors ride horses or learn to use a tomahawk or to develop their speed and strength. Instead, they get educated and learn to use their talent and ability to develop their mind and strengthen their spirit. Warriors constantly grow this way so they can better serve others." Grandpa came over and sat on the porch steps next to Justin.

"Face it, Justin. We're not strong like bears. We can't see like an eagle, hear like a deer or smell like a wolf. If we depended on those abilities to survive, we would have disappeared a long time ago. But we have powerful gifts: our mind and spirit. We can choose to do what we will with these gifts, Justin. But too many people do nothing with them."

Justin's head spun and his heart raced. When the two went into the house to eat dinner, Grandpa's words marinated in Justin's mind. Afterward, Justin grabbed a sheet of paper, went to his room and wrote down the plans he had for his life. Seeing the ideas in black-and-white, he sensed excitement he hadn't felt since childhood. He was nervous. He didn't quite know *how* he'd get there. But he finally knew *what* he wanted—no, *what* he *needed* in his life. He also sensed he now had the courage required to do something about it.

Justin only got a few hours' sleep that night, but he woke up with more energy than ever. With a spring in his step, he waved good-bye to Grandpa and carried only a sheet of paper in his hand. Justin headed down the same sidewalk he had headed down hundreds of times before. However, this time the path was leading him somewhere else—to a place he'd only just begun to imagine.

CHAPTER TEN
Points of Wisdom

- A warrior's power does not lie in his strength, his size or feats in battle. A warrior's power lies in his heart, his character and his commitment to those he serves.

- A warrior's purpose involved developing his abilities to become an asset to the village. Today, that "village" can be your family, community, campus, clients, coworkers— anyone you serve.

- A warrior constantly asks, "What am I doing to develop myself to better care for the people I serve?"

- Warriors no longer ride horses or learn to use a tomahawk. Instead, they get educated to develop their mind and strengthen their spirit so they can better serve others.

- You have powerful gifts: your mind and spirit. You can choose what you will do with these gifts.

- There is a tiny warrior that lives inside us all.

Epilogue

NOW MIDDLE-AGED, Justin sat in a fold-up chair on an outdoor stage. He smiled, thinking of how it reminded him of graduation from State University many years ago. Teased as the oldest freshman in his class, his classmates gave him bronzed dentures when he finally got his diploma. Grandpa never let him live that one down, and Justin always suspected he had something to do with the joke. Since then, Grandpa had passed away. But not a day went by that Justin didn't think about his grandfather's role in changing his life.

The public address system crackled: ". . . earning his engineering degree from State University and later attending business school, he has created a successful family and business. He also serves as a mentor and role model to the youth of our town. He has helped make Solitary the strong and successful community it is today. Ladies and gentlemen, to cut the ribbon on the Tiny Warrior Youth Complex, we bring you the engineer who designed and built it. Justin, please step forward."

Applause exploded as Justin rose from his seat. He

walked over to the podium and struggled to swallow. Looking back at the complex, he appreciated the beauty of the structure, the connected library, the park and—most important—the hundreds of children beaming at him. He proudly cut the ribbon.

"Justin, the tribal council has something for you," the emcee continued. Some of the dignitaries helped an elderly lady with braided hair up from her seat. Her silver earrings swayed as she shuffled slowly over to Justin. In her wrinkled hand she carried a small, rectangular cedar box that had seen better days.

"This is from a friend. I made a promise to give it to you when the time was right," she said in a sweet, raspy voice.

Justin's hands trembled as he took the box. He thumbed the brass hook over and opened the lid. Inside, he found a magnificent, old eagle feather and a handwritten note on yellowed paper:

"Dearest Justin, I always knew he was inside of you, and I thank the Creator that you finally let him out. You have earned this honor. Take care of yourself and continue to nurture your tiny warrior. Love Always, Grandpa."

Final Note

THE PATH OF A WARRIOR is not an easy one. Warriors make mistakes, feel pain, get scared and they cry. Sometimes they fight with all the fury they can muster, only to find out they are fighting themselves. All of this doesn't matter because warriors keep going in spite of it all, in spite of themselves. They persist in fighting to become the person they desperately need to be; a better person for the Creator, for their family, friends, community, coworkers, clients and themselves. Warriors are people like you—and like me.

D. J. Vanas

About the Author

D. **J**. EAGLE BEAR VANAS is a nationally acclaimed motivational speaker and author of Odawa Indian and Dutch descent. He works with organizations that want to develop people and with people who want to raise their level of performance. His experiences as a veteran Sun Dancer, a captain in the U.S. Air Force and a business owner give him powerful insights into boosting performance and breaking through the barriers to success.

He holds a B.S. degree from the U.S. Air Force Academy and an M.S. degree from the University of Southern California. He is one of the few Native American members of the National Speaker's Association and Colorado Speaker's Association.

D.J. owns Native Discovery Inc., a Colorado Springs–based company dedicated to "building the warriors of tomorrow today." His clients include NASA, Hewlett-Packard, the Bureau of Indian Affairs and hundreds of Native American tribes and nations.

D.J.'s passion comes from inspiring others to discover and develop their own gifts to create success in their own lives. His happiness comes from being with his beautiful wife, Arienne, and their priceless treasure, daughter Gabrielle.

For more information or comments, or to schedule a presentation with your group, contact D.J. at:

Native Discovery Inc.
P.O. Box 62657, Colorado Springs, CO 80962
(719) 282-7747, Fax (719) 282-4113
Or visit us at *www.nativediscovery.com*

CHAPTER ONE
Reflections and Breakthroughs

CHAPTER TWO
Reflections and Breakthroughs

CHAPTER THREE
Reflections and Breakthroughs

_____

_____

_____

_____

_____

_____

_____

_____

_____

_____

_____

_____

_____

_____

_____

_____

_____

_____

Reflections and Breakthroughs

_____

_____

_____

_____

_____

_____

_____

_____

_____

_____

_____

_____

_____

_____

_____

_____

_____

_____

_____

Reflections and Breakthroughs

Reflections and Breakthroughs

CHAPTER SEVEN
Reflections and Breakthroughs

_____

_____

_____

_____

_____

_____

_____

_____

_____

_____

_____

_____

_____

_____

_____

_____

_____

_____

_____

Reflections and Breakthroughs

Reflections and Breakthroughs

_____

_____

_____

_____

_____

_____

_____

_____

_____

_____

_____

_____

_____

_____

_____

_____

_____

_____

_____

CHAPTER TEN

Reflections and Breakthroughs